THE STORY OF THE
BLACK NATIONAL
ANTHEM

BY DUCHESS HARRIS, JD, PHD
WITH A. R. CARSER

Core Library

An Imprint of Abdo Publishing
abdobooks.com

Cover image: CeCe Jones-Davis sings the Black
National Anthem before an NBA game in 2017.

abdocorelibrary.com

Published by Abdo Publishing, a division of ABDO, PO Box 398166, Minneapolis, Minnesota 55439. Copyright © 2019 by Abdo Consulting Group, Inc. International copyrights reserved in all countries. No part of this book may be reproduced in any form without written permission from the publisher. Core Library™ is a trademark and logo of Abdo Publishing.

Printed in the United States of America, North Mankato, Minnesota
092018
012019

Cover Photo: Alonzo Adams/AP Images
Interior Photos: Alonzo Adams/AP Images, 1; Andre Chung/MCT/Tribune News Service/Getty Images, 5; Charles Seaver/Florida Memory State Library & Archives, 6–7; Charles H. Phillips/The LIFE Picture Collection/Getty Images, 9; Everett Collection Inc/Alamy, 11; Red Line Editorial, 12, 38; New York Public Library/Science Source, 14–15; Science History Images/Alamy, 17; Everett Historical/Shutterstock Images, 19; Everett Collection/Newscom, 22; AP Images, 24–25, 33, 43; akg-images/Newscom, 28; Shutterstock Images, 30; Don Campbell/The Herald-Palladium/AP Images, 36–37

Editor: Maddie Spalding
Series Designer: Claire Vanden Branden

Library of Congress Control Number: 2018949702

Publisher's Cataloging-in-Publication Data

Names: Harris, Duchess, author. | Carser, A. R., author.
Title: The story of the black national anthem / by Duchess Harris and A. R. Carser.
Description: Minneapolis, Minnesota : Abdo Publishing, 2019 | Series: Freedom's promise | Includes online resources and index.
Identifiers: ISBN 9781532117763 (lib. bdg.) | ISBN 9781641856102 (pbk) | ISBN 9781532170621 (ebook)
Subjects: LCSH: National anthems--Juvenile literature. | National Association for the Advancement of Colored People--Juvenile literature. | Black music (African American music)--Juvenile literature. | African Americans--Poetry--Juvenile literature.
Classification: DDC 782.250--dc23

CONTENTS

A LETTER FROM DUCHESS

The last stanza of the patriotic song "My Country 'Tis of Thee" is *Let freedom ring*. One of the stanzas in "Lift Every Voice and Sing," also known as the Black National Anthem, is *Ring with the harmony of liberty*.

An anthem is a battle cry of freedom. "My Country 'Tis of Thee" was written in the 1830s. It was considered the US national anthem until "The Star Spangled Banner" became the official national anthem in 1931. Between these years, the National Association for the Advancement of Colored People (NAACP) adopted "Lift Every Voice and Sing" as its official song in 1919. It became an anthem for African Americans.

All cultures have anthems. In the African American community, protest songs are embedded in our history. Enslaved black people used them to resist the terror and violence of slavery. Even today, anthems have meaning. *The Story of the Black National Anthem* examines how the Black National Anthem came about and what it means today. Join me on a journey that examines the promise of freedom.

Duchess Harris

People sing the Black National Anthem by the Martin Luther King Jr. Memorial in Washington, DC.

CHAPTER ONE

LIFT
EVERY VOICE

The voices of 500 African American children rang out across the schoolyard of the Stanton School in Jacksonville, Florida. It was February 12, 1900. The school was celebrating President Abraham Lincoln's birthday. The singers dedicated their performance to African American civil rights leader Booker T. Washington.

The school had originally asked principal James Weldon Johnson to write a speech to honor Lincoln. But James came up with a new idea. He decided to write a poem. He discussed his idea with his brother, J. Rosamond Johnson. Rosamond taught music

The Stanton School opened in 1869 and educated hundreds of African American students.

at a college in south Florida. The brothers decided to write a song for the schoolchildren to sing. James would write the poem. Rosamond would set it to music. They called their song "Lift Every Voice and Sing."

In the end, the song was not about Lincoln. It instead celebrated the endurance of African Americans in the face of inequality. The Johnson brothers understood that the work they did served a greater purpose. They believed the purpose of their work was to promote equality and build a sense of community among African Americans.

James Weldon Johnson was both a writer and an activist.

SLAVERY AND SEGREGATION

In 1900 people of African descent were no longer

enslaved in the United States. The American Civil War

had brought an end to slavery. But African Americans

still struggled to be treated equally. They faced discrimination and violence. Segregation kept them legally separated from white people. Black people could not participate in politics and business with their white neighbors. Black communities formed their own schools and social groups. The Stanton School was founded in 1868.

Black students attended separate schools from white students in the early 1900s.

INFLUENTIAL VOICES

PERFORMER	DATE	VENUE/EVENT
Ray Charles	September 18, 1972	The *Dick Cavett Show*
Barack Obama	February 9, 2010	White House Civil Rights Concert
Opera singer Denyce Graves	September 24, 2016	Opening Ceremonies for the National Museum of African American History and Culture in Washington, DC
Beyoncé	April 14, 2018	Coachella Music Festival

"Lift Every Voice and Sing" has been sung by many influential people. The chart above lists notable performances of this song. In what types of settings has this anthem been sung? How does this chart help you understand how important this anthem has been to black people throughout history?

It was the first school opened for African Americans in Florida.

After the public performance of their song, James and Rosamond turned their attention to other work. They both gave little thought to "Lift Every Voice and Sing." But the schoolchildren and their teachers never forgot the words. They sang it at school assemblies and graduations. Students taught their classmates, friends, and families the words. Teachers taught other teachers. The song's uplifting message gave black singers strength and a sense of pride. By 1920 "Lift Every Voice and Sing" had become the anthem of black people across the country.

EXPLORE ONLINE

Chapter One discusses the first performance of "Lift Every Voice and Sing." Since 1900 many artists have performed this song. Read the song lyrics at the website below. Which lines suggest struggle? Which are the most hopeful?

"LIFT EVERY VOICE AND SING"
abdocorelibrary.com/black-national-anthem

CHAPTER
TWO

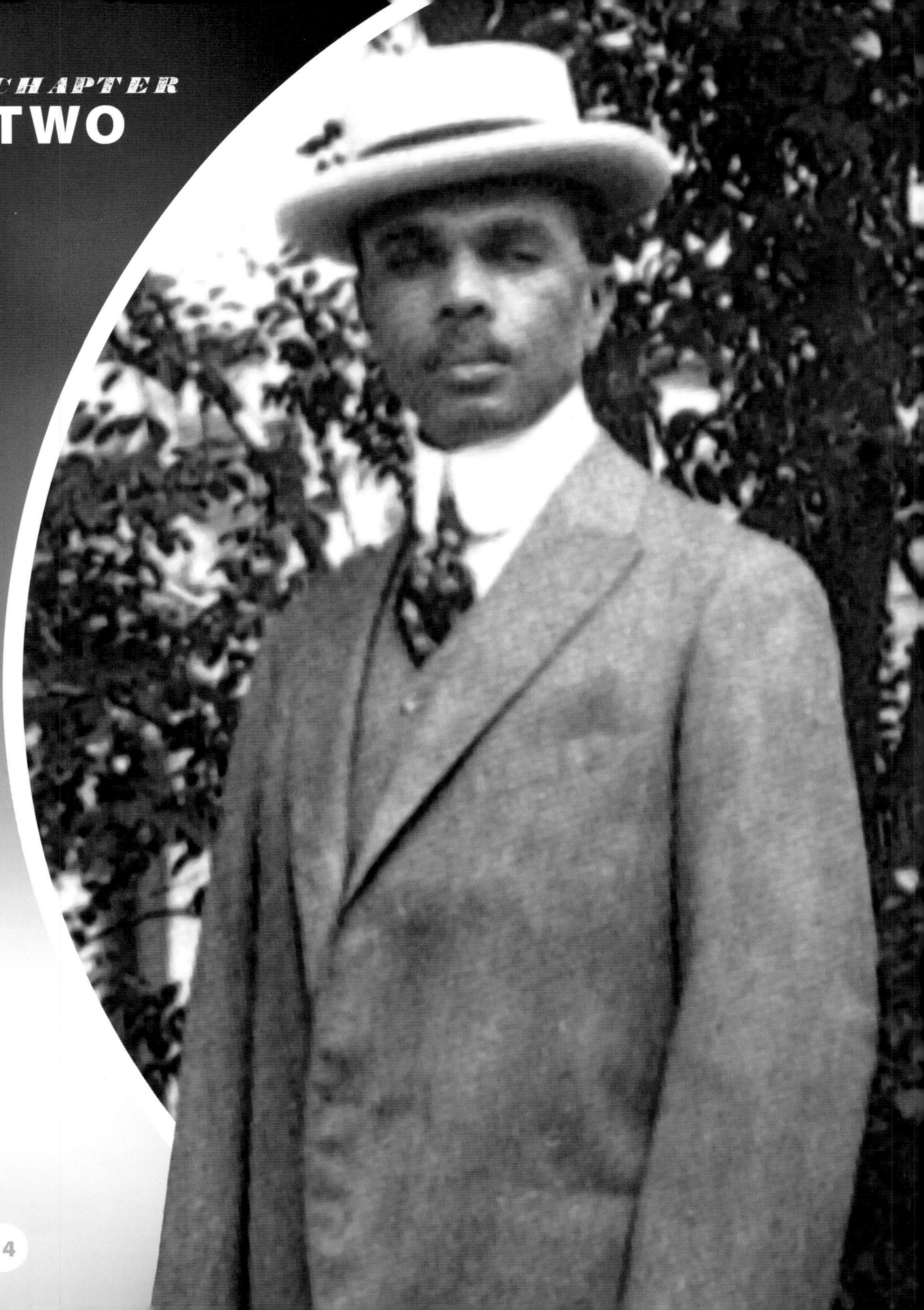

LIFE IN THE JIM CROW SOUTH

James and Rosamond Johnson grew up in Jacksonville. Their mother was an immigrant from the Bahamas. Their father was a freeborn man from Virginia. He worked at a hotel in Jacksonville. Their mother taught at the Stanton School.

After the Civil War, freed African Americans were hopeful they could find jobs. Florida was especially attractive to many black people. Its laws and economy made it easier for black people to own property and find jobs. It also had the first public school system in the South. Still, many black Americans struggled to make a living. The Johnson brothers grew

James Weldon Johnson faced prejudice while growing up in Jacksonville, Florida.

"RACE MEN"

James and Rosamond Johnson believed the work they did served a higher purpose. They wanted the work they did to improve their communities. They wanted their work to motivate people to work toward equality. They considered themselves and others with similar values "race men." Their careers did not just support themselves and their families. They were in service of all African Americans.

up in a middle-class household. It was unusual for black Americans to make it into the middle class at the time.

James was born in 1871. Rosamond was born two years later. Their parents encouraged the boys to express themselves through writing, music, and other arts. James attended the Stanton School. He went on to graduate from Atlanta University. He later became a teacher and principal at the Stanton School. Rosamond studied music at the New England Conservatory in Boston, Massachusetts. He began his career as a music teacher while James taught at the Stanton School. James later studied the law with a

J. Rosamond Johnson, *left*, played piano and toured with singer Taylor Gordon, *right*, in the 1920s.

white attorney named Thomas Ledwith. James became an attorney himself in 1898. Running the school and studying law took up a lot of James's time. But he still wrote music and poetry.

James and Rosamond moved to New York City in 1901. They hoped to write songs for musicals. James and Rosamond were not alone in their migration north. Many African Americans had moved out of the South in search of better opportunities. The late 1800s and early 1900s were difficult times for African Americans. Federal and state governments restricted the rights of African Americans, especially in the South.

PRESIDENTIAL RECONSTRUCTION

The Confederacy broke up after the Civil War ended in 1865. The Confederacy was the group of states that tried to break away from the United States in the Civil War. They wanted to continue the practice of slavery. After they lost the war, they rejoined the United States. The US Congress passed the Thirteenth Amendment to end slavery. For the next 12 years, the federal government took steps to rebuild southern society. These years were known as the Reconstruction period.

Andrew Johnson was the US president during Reconstruction. President Johnson allowed southerners to reconstruct their society. Southern states enacted laws called the Black Codes. These laws restricted the types of jobs available to black people. They allowed states to hire out black children and orphans to white

Andrew Johnson became president after Abraham Lincoln was assassinated in 1865.

landowners. African Americans were not allowed to testify in court. They could not carry guns.

RECONSTRUCTION IN THE NORTH

President Johnson was unpopular in the North. Many northerners disliked the Black Codes. In 1866 the Radical Republican political party took control of Congress. This party had opposed slavery. It took action against the former Confederacy. Congress ended the

Black Codes and passed the Civil Rights Bill. This law declared all people born in the United States national citizens. It said that all people had equal rights under the law. This included African Americans.

PERSPECTIVES
PRESIDENT JOHNSON

Andrew Johnson became president in 1865. Johnson came from the South. He had refused to join the Confederate cause in 1861. But he believed states had the right to create their own laws about slavery. He allowed southern states to create their own laws at the end of the Civil War. But going easy on southern states proved to be unpopular. Johnson failed to win his party's nomination to become a presidential candidate in 1868. He left office in 1869.

The Fourteenth Amendment was later passed in 1868. It said that former slaves should be granted citizenship and given equal protection under the law. In 1870 Congress passed the Fifteenth Amendment. This amendment gave black men the right to vote. Black people began to exercise their new rights. Black men registered to vote. They participated in elections. Many also ran for office. Black men and women started newspapers for black audiences.

Many white communities did not welcome the new success of black communities. This included white communities in the South and in the North. Support for Reconstruction began to decline. Violence against African Americans increased in the South. By 1877 the federal government had stopped protecting the rights of black people. Reconstruction had come to an end.

THE NADIR

Beginning in the late 1800s, southern states enacted Jim Crow laws. The term "Jim Crow" came from a racist character played by a white actor in the early 1800s. Jim Crow laws kept black men from voting. They forced African Americans into low-wage jobs. They made racial segregation legal in the South. African Americans were barred from entering many public spaces.

In the Jim Crow south, black people were segregated in many public places, including bus stations.

Violence against black people increased. This violence often went unpunished by law enforcement. Historians call this time period the nadir of race relations in the United States. A nadir is the lowest point of something. Many people believe this time period was the lowest point in the relations between black and white people in the United States.

FIGHTING RACISM

Jim Crow laws did not stop black communities from organizing. Between the 1870s and early 1900s, more than 1,200 African American newspapers existed. James ran one called the *Daily American*. African Americans also founded schools. These schools hired black teachers and taught black students. Rosamond and other musicians wrote music for black audiences. Their music reflected black experiences and culture. James and other black writers wrote literature for black audiences.

Racism was ever present in the Jim Crow South. James and Rosamond fought against racism. They promoted equality. They wrote "Lift Every Voice and Sing" with this purpose in mind. It was a mission that would become more important to the brothers in the 1900s.

FURTHER EVIDENCE

Chapter Two talks about the time periods before and after Reconstruction. What is one of the main points of this chapter? What evidence does the author provide to support this point? Read the article at the website below. Does the information on the website support this point? Or does it present new evidence?

THE BOOKER T. WASHINGTON ERA

abdocorelibrary.com/black-national-anthem

CHAPTER THREE

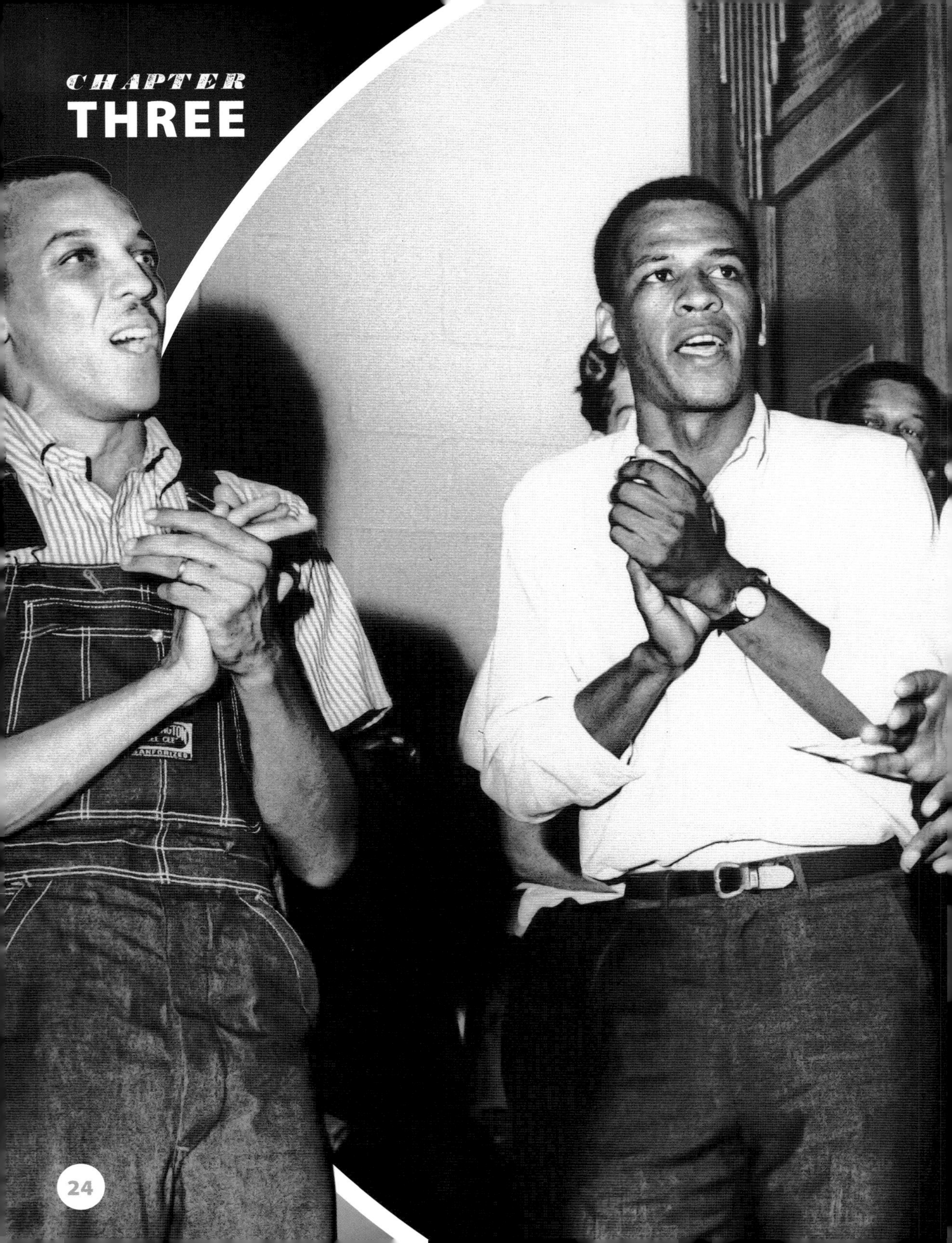

FREEDOM SONGS

The Johnson brothers' song quickly became popular in the early 1900s. In 1901 Victoria Earle Matthews called "Lift Every Voice and Sing" an anthem for black people. Matthews was a leader of the National Association of Colored Women's Clubs (NACWC). The NACWC organized women's clubs across the country. Each club included women who were important to their communities. Teachers and church leaders joined women's clubs. Activists joined these clubs too. They shared Matthews's message with their friends and family. The song spread to black communities across the South.

Freedom songs, such as the Black National Anthem, were popular at civil rights meetings in the 1960s.

HISTORICAL TERMS

Naming customs for groups of people are constantly changing. A term that was used in one time period may become insensitive or offensive in another. From the Reconstruction period through the civil rights era, the word *negro* was often used to refer to a black person. African American organizations such as the Negro Literary and History Society of Atlanta used this term in their names. The term *colored* was also used at the time to refer to a black person. But public opinion of these words has changed over time. Today some Americans of African descent prefer the term *African American*. Others prefer *black*.

In 1903 the Negro Literary and History Society of Atlanta held a ceremony. The ceremony celebrated the signing of the Emancipation Proclamation in 1863. The Emancipation Proclamation was an order that declared enslaved people in the South to be free. This did not end slavery. But it did give enslaved people hope that they would soon be free. On Emancipation Day in 1903, attendees at the ceremony sang "Lift Every Voice and Sing." The song spoke to the struggles of enslaved people. But it also gave people pride at having faced and overcome obstacles. It gave them hope for a better future.

A HIGHER PURPOSE

James Johnson became secretary of the National Association for the Advancement of Colored People (NAACP) in 1916. The NAACP advocates for equality for African Americans. James helped open new branches of the NAACP. He also helped the organization gain more members. He led the NAACP's efforts to combat racism and segregation. He resigned from the NAACP in 1930. He became a creative writing teacher at Fisk University in Tennessee.

In 1919 the NAACP adopted "Lift Every Voice and Sing" as its official song. The NAACP printed copies of the music. It distributed the copies to black communities across the country. At the time, violence against African Americans was becoming more widespread. White mobs lynched 70 African Americans

The NAACP organized protests to fight segregation and other inequalities.

in 1919. Eleven more African Americans were burned to death. The NAACP wanted to share the song's message with all African Americans. The song acknowledged the violence and danger faced by black people. It gave them the strength to keep fighting for equality.

THE GREAT MIGRATION

Black schools in the South were run by African Americans. These schools were free to create their own traditions. Most adopted "Lift Every Voice and Sing" as their official anthem. Students sang it in classes and at assemblies. The words and lyrics of the song were taught in English and music classes. This generation of students would grow up to become leaders in the civil rights movement.

Violence and a lack of job opportunities in the South caused many African Americans to move north. Between 1910 and 1920, 1.6 million African Americans moved from the South to the North. This movement was known as the Great Migration. The populations of African Americans in many urban areas doubled or even tripled. Families settled in northern cities such as New York City. When African Americans moved north, they brought "Lift Every Voice and Sing" with them. The song became part of the identity of black communities in the North. It inspired the work of activists, leaders, and artists.

In the early 1900s, the arts flourished in Harlem. Harlem is a mostly black neighborhood in New York City where many artists and musicians live. This time period

Many singers and musicians performed at the Apollo Theater in Harlem during the Harlem Renaissance.

became known as the Harlem Renaissance. Black writers and artists flocked to Harlem. The Johnson brothers lived in Harlem at the time. They wrote approximately 200 songs for Broadway musicals. They helped pave the way for a new era of African American art.

THE FIGHT FOR EQUALITY

The fight for African Americans to secure equal rights was known as the civil rights movement. In the 1950s and 1960s, civil rights work became more urgent. African Americans had served the United States in two world wars. They had fought for their country overseas.

But at home, they still faced Jim Crow laws and mob violence.

In December 1955, Rosa Parks was riding a bus in Montgomery, Alabama. The bus driver told her to give up her seat to a white man. She refused and was arrested. Parks's arrest sparked outrage. Five days later, Martin Luther King Jr. and other activists led a boycott of the Montgomery bus system. The boycott lasted more than a year. Getting around town without public transportation was difficult.

PERSPECTIVES
KING'S SPEECHES

Martin Luther King Jr. sometimes included "Lift Every Voice and Sing" in his sermons and speeches. He quoted a line from the song when he gave his first speech in 1944. In 1957 he gave a speech to mark the anniversary of the Emancipation Proclamation. The melody of "Lift Every Voice and Sing" played in the background during part of his speech. King also used the lyrics in a speech during a 1965 march in Selma, Alabama. The march drew attention to the death of black civil rights activist Jimmie Lee Jackson. The song's lyrics helped rally protesters.

Continuing the boycott required organization and endurance. Throughout the boycott, churches and organizers relied on "Lift Every Voice and Sing" to renew their sense of purpose. In December 1956, the US Supreme Court ruled that racial segregation on buses violated the Fourteenth Amendment. Segregated seating was no longer legal.

Over the next 20 years, students and other activist groups organized across the South. These groups wanted to desegregate institutions that had been exclusively white. This included schools and the government. They staged sit-ins at businesses that refused to serve black people. They organized marches to fight for equal rights. Their work persuaded many white Americans that change was needed. In 1964 President Lyndon B. Johnson signed the Civil Rights Act into law. This act enforced desegregation and outlawed discrimination. But black people in the South still faced obstacles that prevented them from voting. They were often forced to pay a tax or take literacy tests before

President Lyndon B. Johnson signed the Voting Rights Act on August 6, 1965.

they were allowed to vote. In 1965 President Johnson signed the Voting Rights Act into law. This law ended these restrictions.

Freedom songs inspired civil rights workers across the country. These songs helped activists feel a sense of community. At first "Lift Every Voice and Sing" continued to be sung at civil rights meetings. But in the 1960s, other freedom songs became more popular. Activists were inspired by songs such as "We Shall Overcome." These songs' melodies were simpler than that of "Lift Every Voice and Sing." They were easier to sing and chant during protests. Some activists blended the lyrics from "Lift Every Voice and Sing" with other freedom songs. But few groups sang the anthem at meetings or during protests.

Despite its fall in popularity, "Lift Every Voice and Sing" continued to be a song of comfort. On April 4, 1968, King was assassinated. At a rally honoring King in Massachusetts, the crowd sang "Lift Every Voice and Sing." By the late 1960s, a new style of African American activism had risen. It was called the Black Power movement. This movement fought against white power structures that enforced racism. It reclaimed "Lift Every Voice and Sing" as a song of protest and pride. By the 1970s, "Lift Every Voice and Sing" had become widely known as the Black National Anthem.

STRAIGHT TO THE
SOURCE

Mildred Johnson Edwards was Rosamond Johnson's daughter. She founded an elementary school in Harlem called the Modern School. She once reflected on the significance of "Lift Every Voice and Sing":

During my childhood in a home filled with music, the hymn written by my father and uncle was merely one among many compositions played and enjoyed by all; however, on my own as an adult I have invoked the song's muse on innumerable occasions. . . . [When] I founded the Modern School . . . "Lift Every Voice and Sing" was used for all official school functions and assembly. It was apparent that the song would be of great help as we strove to foster a sense of heritage and pride for the primarily African American pupils.

Source: Mildred Johnson Edwards. *Lift Every Voice and Sing: A Celebration of the Negro National Anthem*. Ed. Julian Bond and Sondra Kathryn Wilson. New York: Random House, 2000. Print. 80.

Consider Your Audience

Adapt this passage for a different audience, such as your teacher or friends. Write a blog post conveying this same information for the new audience. How does your post differ from the original text and why?

CHAPTER FOUR

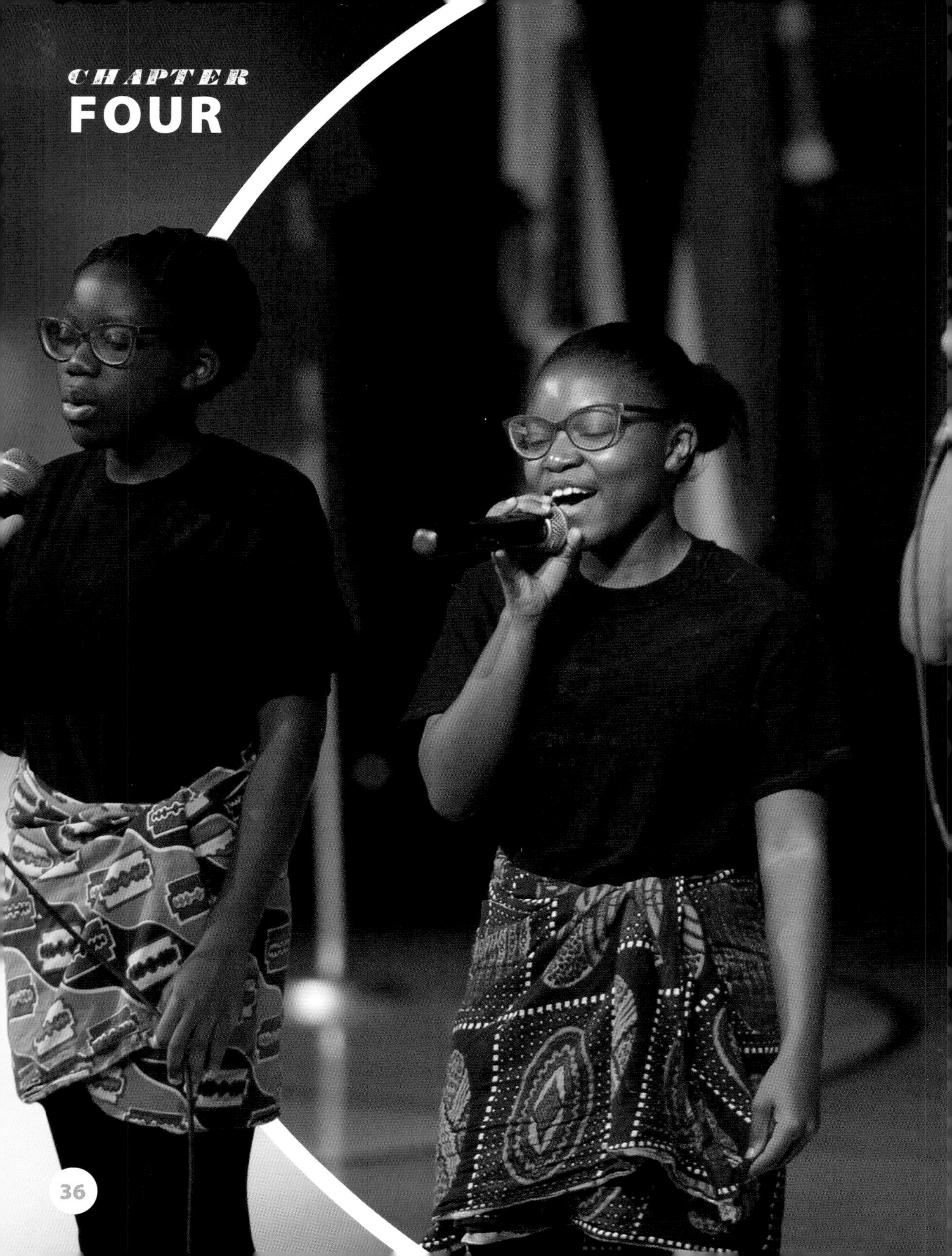

LIFTING MODERN VOICES

The Civil Rights Act had a dramatic effect on the South. Jim Crow was no longer the law of the land. White schools were forced to integrate. White and black students now attended the same schools. Integration also happened in other public spaces. The hard work of millions of people had made this change possible. Through it all, they had sung "Lift Every Voice and Sing."

Students perform "Lift Every Voice and Sing" during an assembly at a high school in Michigan.

CIVIL RIGHTS TIMELINE

1909
The NAACP
is founded.

1964
The Civil Rights Act
makes segregation
illegal. It gives black
people equal rights
under the law.

2014
People in Ferguson,
Missouri, protest
the police killing of
Michael Brown.

1900
James and
Rosamond
Johnson write
"Lift Every Voice
and Sing."

1955
Rosa Parks is
arrested for refusing
to give up her seat
on a bus to a white
man. Her arrest
leads to the
Montgomery bus
boycott.

1968
Martin Luther
King Jr. is
assassinated.

"Lift Every Voice and Sing" continues to be a song of activism and hope for black communities. The timeline above lists a few major civil rights events. How did the Black National Anthem lift up black communities during these time periods?

EFFECTS OF INTEGRATION

As black students integrated into white schools, the tradition of singing "Lift Every Voice and Sing" at school was left behind. In the early 1900s, most African Americans knew the words to "Lift Every Voice and Sing." But by the 1980s, its popularity had declined.

One group of institutions has kept the tradition alive. Historically black colleges and universities (HBCUs) are African American schools that were established before the Civil Rights Act of 1964. HBCUs educated black students. "Lift Every Voice and Sing" continues to be performed at HBCUs such as Tuskegee University today.

THE ANTHEM TODAY

Recent police violence against African Americans has prompted a revival of "Lift Every Voice and Sing." In 2014 a white police officer shot and killed Michael Brown. Brown was an unarmed black teenager. The shooting occurred in Ferguson, Missouri. Protests after the shooting lasted for days. Some protesters sang "Lift Every Voice and Sing."

HBCUs

Colleges and universities became integrated after the Civil Rights Act of 1964. Before then many colleges barred African Americans from attending. There are 101 HBCUs across the country. HBCUs gave black people the opportunity to earn degrees at a time when many other colleges did not. Graduates of HBCUs have become professors, engineers, lawyers, judges, and members of Congress.

In 2015 a black man named Freddie Gray died while in police custody in Baltimore, Maryland. The Baltimore Symphony Orchestra put on a special concert. Its program included a sing-along version of "Lift Every Voice and Sing."

"Lift Every Voice and Sing" has strengthened and inspired people for more than 100 years.

Today a new generation of African Americans continues to fight for equality. They will define the future role "Lift Every Voice and Sing" will have in civil rights work.

STRAIGHT TO THE
SOURCE

Dr. Tim Askew is an African American professor at Clark Atlanta University. He believes that calling "Lift Every Voice and Sing" the Black National Anthem is inaccurate. He thinks the song speaks to the experiences of all people. In a 2015 interview, he said:

> What I found was this whole mythology that all black people have associated "Lift Every Voice and Sing" as a black national anthem is just simply not true. . . . Many African Americans have been in conflict about this whole idea of a song being a black national anthem. If you want equality and civil rights and human rights, how can you have a song with that kind of label because that's not the kind of label that brings blacks and whites and all other races together.

> Source: Kate Lochte and Matt Markgraf. "MSU Lecture: 'Lift Every Voice and Sing' an Analysis of the 'Black National Anthem.'" *WKMS*. Murray State University, March 24, 2015. Web. Accessed March 31, 2018.

Point of View
Askew discusses why some people may not want to call "Lift Every Voice and Sing" the Black National Anthem. What reasons does he give? Read back through this chapter. Do you agree? Why or why not?

FAST FACTS

- Brothers James and Rosamond Johnson wrote "Lift Every Voice and Sing." The song was first performed at the Stanton School in Florida on February 12, 1900.

- By 1901 "Lift Every Voice and Sing" had started to spread to African American communities across the South.

- The NAACP adopted "Lift Every Voice and Sing" as its official song in 1919.

- In 1955 Rosa Parks was arrested for refusing to give up her seat to a white man. Her arrest led to the Montgomery bus boycott. Organizers sang "Lift Every Voice and Sing" to keep up people's spirits during the boycott.

- By the 1970s, "Lift Every Voice and Sing" had become widely known as the Black National Anthem.

- "Lift Every Voice and Sing" continues to be sung today. Students at historically black colleges and universities sing it to honor its importance in the black community. Protesters sing it to bring attention to injustices against African Americans.

STOP AND THINK

Why Do I Care?

The era of Jim Crow is over. But that doesn't mean issues of racism, discrimination, and inequality have gone away. How does the civil rights movement affect your life today? Are there laws that might not exist without it?

Take a Stand

The US national anthem is often played in schools and before sporting events. The US national anthem is better known among the public than the Black National Anthem. Do you think the Black National Anthem should be played more often during public events? Why or why not?

Tell the Tale

Chapter Three discusses how "Lift Every Voice and Sing" was used during the civil rights movement. Imagine you were at a civil rights protest where people sang this song. Write 200 words about your experience. What messages were people trying to communicate with this song?

GLOSSARY

anthem
a song of praise and pride

boycott
an organized refusal to use products or services as a form of protest

discrimination
the unjust treatment of a person or group based on race or other perceived differences

integrate
to include people of all races in a group in an attempt to give them equal rights and protection under the law

lynched
murdered by a mob or group of people

racism
a belief that a certain race is better than others

segregation
the separation of people of different races or ethnic groups through separate schools and other public spaces

sit-in
a type of organized protest where activists sit in the seats or on the floor of businesses that refuse to serve them

ONLINE RESOURCES

To learn more about the Black National Anthem, visit our free resource websites below.

Visit **abdocorelibrary.com** for free Common Core resources for teachers and students, including vetted activities, multimedia, and booklinks, for deeper subject comprehension.

Visit **abdobooklinks.com** for free additional online weblinks for further learning. These links are routinely monitored and updated to provide the most current information available.

LEARN MORE

Harris, Duchess. *Civil Rights Sit-Ins*. Minneapolis, MN: Abdo Publishing, 2018.

Terp, Gail. *Nonviolent Resistance in the Civil Rights Movement*. Minneapolis, MN: Abdo Publishing, 2016.

ABOUT THE
AUTHORS

Duchess Harris, JD, PhD

Professor Harris is the chair of the American Studies department at Macalester College and curator of the Duchess Harris Collection of ABDO books. She is the author and coauthor of recently released ABDO books including *Hidden Human Computers: The Black Women of NASA*, *Black Lives Matter*, and *Race and Policing*.

Before working with ABDO, she authored several other books on the topics of race, culture, and American history. She served as an associate editor for *Litigation News*, the American Bar Association Section of Litigation's quarterly flagship publication, and was the first editor in chief of *Law Raza*, an interactive online journal covering race and the law, published at William Mitchell College of Law. She has earned a PhD in American Studies from the University of Minnesota and a JD from William Mitchell College of Law.

A. R. Carser

A. R. Carser is a freelance writer who lives in Minnesota. She enjoys learning and writing about US history, culture, and society.

INDEX